Finding the Joy
In Everyday Living

Finding the Joy
In Everyday Living

Stories and Insights for Living
A More Fulfilled Life

Third Edition

Rabbi Pesach Scheiner

Hafatzoh Publishing
Boulder, Colorado
2012

Copyright © 2012 by Pesach Scheiner

First edition. All rights reserved.

No part of this book may be reproduced or transmitted in any form or by any means, electronic or mechanical, including photocopy, recording, or any information storage or retrieval system, except for brief passages in connection with a critical review, without permission in writing from the publisher:

Hafatzoh Publishing
4740 Table Mesa Dr. Suite B
Boulder, CO 80305
303-494-1638

Design and composition by Albion-Andalus, Inc.
Cover design by Daryl McCool.

Manufactured in the United States of America

ISBN: 1453889124

EAN-13: 9781453889121

Dedication

This book is dedicated to our parents, Rabbi Mordechai and Rivka Scheiner, and Rabbi Gerson and Lea Chanowitz; they are our guides in life, and we wish them many blessings in theirs.

— Pesach & Chany Scheiner

Contents

Acknowledgments
Finding Your Joy   11

I. The Art of Contentment   15
II. The Art of Meaning   27
III. The Art of Friendship   47
IV. The Art of Marriage   61
V. The Art of Thinking   73
VI. The Art of Attitude   95
VII. The Art of Giving   115
VIII. The Art of Faith   131

Bibliography
About the Author

Acknowledgements

I wish to give a heartfelt thank you to the people who helped to make this book a reality. Firstly, to my wife Chany, who spent a lot of time helping me develop the material. Secondly, to Netanel Miles-Yépez who, besides being a fantastic editor, was also instrumental in creating the pleasing format of the book.

Although this book is compiled from many sources, there is much material from Dr. Morris Mandel, of blessed memory, who wrote popular columns in *The Jewish Press* for many years. He was a great teacher who guided many people towards a better life and I am extremely grateful to him.

— P.S.

Finding Your Joy

Everybody desires happiness, and yet, ironically, many people have a major misconception about what it means to live a happy and fulfilled life. Some are of the opinion that happiness is a feeling of joy and ecstasy associated with special occasions. They believe that the key to living a fulfilled life is to have as many of these occasions as possible. Thus, they go on vacation as often as they can and purchase as many exciting luxuries as they can afford, and often more than they can afford.

But if this is the definition of happiness, then happiness is basically reduced to a feeling of excitement and pleasure. So what happens when those things begin to lose their novelty and cease to excite us as they initially did? For it is a law of nature that they almost certainly do before long.

So how should we define happiness? Happiness is the feeling of joy we have when we are feeling *good*. For when we feel *good*, then even mundane tasks are accompanied by joyous feelings. For example, when you wake-up after a good night's sleep, feeling well-rested and energized, you might spend the morning doing chores, but they are often accompanied by a feeling of well-being. Likewise, when you *do* something good, a feeling of joy and contentment pervades the rest of your activities.

How can we experience happiness and fulfillment on a regular basis?

The answer is by keeping both our body and spirit healthy. As human beings, we are comprised of both a body and a soul or spirit, and we have to pay attention to the health of each. Just as the body needs certain nutrients, the human spirit has emotional needs. But just as there are things we ingest that are damaging to the body, there are also certain emotions that are damaging to the human spirit.

Allow me to illustrate with a story:

There was once a man who sought medical attention because he had popped eyes and a ringing in his ears. He went from doctor to doctor, and each of them, after a thorough examination, gave him a different prescription. One urged him to have his teeth removed, another to take out his tonsils, a third insisted that his appendix was the cause of his troubles. He listened to all of them and had half of his body removed—but his eyes still popped and his ears still rang. Desperate, he decided to see one more specialist, who told him that he had only six months to live.

That being the case, he decided that he might as well have a good time while he was still able to enjoy it. He bought an expensive car, reserved a suite in the best hotel, and decided to have an entire wardrobe custom-made for him by a tailor.

The tailor said to him, "Just let me get your measurements . . . Okay, thirty-four sleeve . . . Sixteen collar."

"No," the man corrected him, "fifteen collar."

The tailor measured again, "Sixteen collar."

"But I have always worn a fifteen collar," the man argued, "and that's how I want it made."

The tailor shrugged. "Okay, but I warn you—you keep wearing a fifteen collar on that sixteen inch neck and your eyes will pop and you'll have ringing in your ears!"[1]

This story might be seen as a metaphor for our search for happiness. Like the man in our story, we often look too far afield for help in finding our happiness. We buy big houses and fancy cars, but we quickly become used to them and realize that we are no more happy than we were before. Then, one day, we come to the realization that we were looking too far outside ourselves for an answer, for some extraordinary thing or explanation, when the real answer was right before us, we are living a lifestyle that

---

[1] Retold from Morris Mandel and Aaron J. Novick, *Walk With Me to Happiness*, 13.

doesn't suit our bodies or our spirits. In this book, we will prescribe a simple diet for healthy living, illustrated by relevant stories, quotations, and insights.

The Art of Contentment

I

*"Success is getting what you want.
Happiness is wanting what you get."*
— Dale Carnegie

On Loving What You Do

Consider the following story on loving what you do by Mrs. Simcha Fine, a Chabad emissary in Montreal:

My father was eighty-two years old when he passed away. He was clear-minded and active until the very end.

He had only retired a year before—voluntarily at the age of eighty-one—and only because my mother wasn't feeling well. There was only one thing that could have torn my father away from a job that he loved so much—and stayed with for over sixty years. He did it for the sake of my mother. Because he would do anything for my mother.

My father was the longest-standing employee at McDonnell Douglas Aircraft. He started building airplanes with McDonnell Douglas when they built them by hand, with sheet metal and hand-held riveters. He was a treasure-trove of stories about the early days of aviation and airplane manufacturing. With great relish, he told us again and again about the experimental planes he worked on. Test-flying them, adjusting them, and then putting them back up into the air again.

When WWII rolled around, my father wanted to sign up to fight. But, as we children knew so well, my father's bosses refused to let him go—he was needed to help build the planes that helped win the war.

And as the aviation industry evolved, so did my father's job. The tasks were taken over by machines, then by computers. Through it all, my father learned to do his job in the new way, to see his tasks from the new perspective.

Sixty-two years at the same desk, the same job. And—as he told us so often—he never had a dull day at the job. He looked forward to going to work each day, and he truly loved every aspect of it. He also looked forward to coming home every day to his wife and seven children. This he didn't have to tell us.

Growing up, the fact that my father loved his work was something I knew about my father, but didn't think was unusual. It was only later that I realized how truly unique this is.

At my father's funeral, my brother spoke about this. He told us that in his early twenties he himself started looking for a job. But he didn't want just any job. He wanted a job like my father's: one he would love; one that would be so interesting that he would never have a boring day; one that he would want to stay with his whole life.

And after years of going from job to job, and being disappointed time after time—he woke up one morning and realized, it's not the job, it's me. It was my father's attitude toward his job that made it wonderful, interesting, and a long-term commitment.

Instead of finding something that he loved, and then doing it, my father took what he had to do, and then loved it.[2]

Sparks of Wisdom

Often, important parts of our lives—like our jobs and personal relationships—have a mixture of good and bad elements in them. Sometimes we get so 'hung-up' on the negative, so challenged by difficulties at work or stresses at home, that it clouds our ability to see what is good in our lives.

---

[2] Reprinted with permission from Mrs. Simcha Fine and the *N'shei Chabad Newsletter* (www.nsheichabadnewsletter.com).

But this failure to take into account the positive elements of the situation makes it a lot harder to deal successfully with the situation as a whole. If we would only stop and count our blessings in the midst of our difficulties, then we might find the way through them with more clarity.

When you are faced with life's difficulties,
Stop and look for the good in your life,
Then keep it in mind as you deal
With your difficulty.

II

"Who is rich?
One who is happy with their lot."
— Rabbi Shimon ben Zoma[3]

How Big is Your Problem?

The famous Persian poet, Saadi, tells us that he never complained about his condition in life except once, when he was barefoot and had no money to buy shoes. Then he happened upon man without feet, and he thanked G-d[4] for his bare feet and was content once again.

> An unknown poet
> Penned these wise words:
> I cannot count my wealth in gold;
> But what is gold to me?
> I've legs for walking, hands for work,

---

[3] Mishnah, Avot 4:1.

[4] This convention for writing the word 'G-d' is used by many Jews in order to preserve the sanctity of the divine name.

> I've eyes with which to see;
> I've lots of gold in memories
> Which money cannot buy;
> There's many a wealthy man today,
> Who's poorer far than I.[5]

Sparks of Wisdom

Life's many little problems have a way of robbing us of our peace of mind. But when we really take the time to look at the 'big picture,' most of these problems don't seem so significant.

The next time you are bothered by a problem you are having, try this little exercise: give it a number between 1 and 10—1 representing a very small problem, and 10 representing a massive problem. If you do this for a while, you'll soon begin to see that most of life's problems don't get a very high number.

Keep your problems in perspective.
Most of them only affect a small part of your life.

---

[5] Retold (and quoted) from Morris Mandel, *Stories to Live By*.

III

"A person does not know what is in the heart of his friend."

Those Who Have it Better

Once, a fisherman on the Mediterranean sat in his little boat, gazing at the splendor of a magnificent palace on the shore. Just then, the prince, whose palace it was, appeared on the balcony, and the fisherman, seeing him surrounded by such splendor, envied him, saying: "Oh, I wish I were that prince! A beautiful palace, delicious foods, and servants to wait on him—What a life!"

At that very moment, the prince on the balcony looked out on the fisherman afar off on the water, and thought: "Oh, I wish I were that fisherman—no worries, no problems, no responsibilities—just a little boat to relax in while I fish!"[6]

---

[6] Retold from Morris Mandel, *Stories to Live By*.

Sparks of Wisdom

One of the major obstacles to contentment is the nagging thought that someone else has it better. The problem is, we are always judging this from our own narrow vantage-point and forgetting that each one of us has our own unique challenges, and our own unique gifts which are shared by no one else. It is not for us to give away our G-d given gifts any more than we can assume another's responsibilities.

Don't let what someone else has
Take away your appreciation for what you have.

IV

"A person who has a hundred dollars, wants two hundred dollars; if they get two hundred dollars, then they want four hundred dollars . . ."

Chasing Happiness

Once, an old dog watched a young dog chasing its tail and asked, "Why are you chasing your tail?"

The young dog said, "Well, I am a student of philosophy, and I have learned that the best thing for a dog is happiness, and being a dog, I know that happiness is my tail. Therefore, I am chasing it! And when I catch it, I will have found happiness."

Then the old dog said, "My son, I have also thought about the problems of the universe in my simple way, and I too have seen that happiness is a fine thing for a dog, and that happiness is in my tail; but I have also noticed that when I chase after it, it keeps running away from me, and when I go about my business, it somehow comes after me."[7]

Sparks of Wisdom

The person who is always wanting 'more' in life will end up (like the young dog in our story) always chasing after happiness. For as soon as that person gets what they want, a new desire comes along to take its place, and thus their appetite is never sated. So how is happiness to be found? Happiness comes as a by-product of living a wholesome life, and by being content with what you have.

Those who always crave for more,
Always feel like they are missing something.

---

[7] Retold from Morris Mandel, *Stories to Live By*.

The Art of Meaning

I

"The world is like a big shop window in which some prankster switched the price tags on the merchandise; the items of lesser value have high prices, and the truly precious items have pitifully low prices."

The Lubavitcher Rebbe's Regards

In the early 1990's, an elderly woman walked into the office of Rabbi Jacob Biederman, who was the Lubavitcher Rebbe's emissary in Vienna, Austria at the time. She introduced herself as Margareta Chayos, a retired opera singer, adding with a smile, "the Lubavitcher Rebbe's *first* emissary in Vienna!"

Thus, she began a long and amazing story. On her mother's side, she was related to the holy Rebbe's of Vizhnitz, but she had grown up in a more secular home in Chernovitz. Eventually, she traveled to Vienna—then one of the cultural centers of the world—and became a successful opera singer. She even performed Mozart before Hitler (who did not know that she was Jewish) in Salzburg in 1939 before being smuggled out of Austria.

In time, she and her husband settled in Detroit, Michigan, where they raised their daughter and began to rebuild their lives. When she was grown, Margareta's daughter married a prominent Jewish doctor, who sometime after was honored at a fundraising dinner for Chabad institutions in New York. Margareta decided to attend this fundraiser, and a private audience was arranged for her with the Lubavitcher Rebbe, Rabbi Menachem Mendel Schneerson.

"I walked into the Rebbe's room," she told Rabbi Biederman, "and I cannot explain why, but suddenly, for the first time since the Holocaust, I felt that I could cry. Like so many others who have lost entire families and communities—I had never cried before. We knew that if we would start crying, we might never stop, or that in order to survive we couldn't express our emotions. But at that moment, it was as though the dam obstructing my inner waterfall of tears was removed. I began sobbing like a baby. I shared with the Rebbe my entire story."

"The Rebbe listened with his eyes, with his heart, with his soul, and he took it all in. I shared everything and he absorbed everything. That night I felt like I was given a second father. I felt that the Rebbe adopted me as his daughter."

At the end of their meeting, she told the Rebbe about her desire to go back and visit Vienna, and the Rebbe asked that she visit him again before making the trip.

A few months later, she visited the Rebbe again as promised, and he asked her to give his regards to two people while she was in Vienna. The first was the Chief Rabbi, Akiva Eisenberg, and the second was a Jewish professor at the University of Vienna. The Rebbe said: "His name is Dr. Frankl. Send him my regards and tell him in my name that he should not give up. He must remain strong and continue his work with vigor and passion. If he continues to remain strong he will prevail."

This seemed like a very strange request, but she decided to do exactly as the Rebbe had asked.

When she got to Vienna, the meeting with Rabbi Eisenberg happened very easily, but the meeting with the professor did not seem likely. For when she went to the university, she was told that professor Frankl had not shown up for classes in two weeks! She tried the university a few more times, but always came away disappointed.

She wanted to give up, but simply couldn't fail the Rebbe. So she decided to violate the usual protocols of Austrian courtesy, to look up the professor's private address and to knock on the door.

A woman answered her knock and she asked if the professor was at home. The woman told her to wait, and a few moments later, a middle-aged man came to the door. He was extremely tense, and looked quite uninterested in what she might have to say.

Feeling more than a little awkward, she said, "I have regards from Rabbi Schneerson in Brooklyn, New York. "

"Who is this?" he asked somewhat curtly.

"Rabbi Schneerson asked me to tell you in his name that you must not give up. You ought to remain strong and continue your work with unflinching determination and you will prevail. Do not fall into despair. If you march on with confidence, he promised that you will achieve great success."

Much to her surprise, the professor's demeanor changed completely. He looked as if he had seen a ghost; his eyes opened wide and his jaw dropped in disbelief. His body began to shake all over, and he put his face in his hands and broke down sobbing like a child!

When he finally recovered, he asked her to come in, and kept saying, "I cannot believe this!" After they sat down, he dried his eyes and said: "This rabbi from Brooklyn knew exactly when to send you here. It is a true miracle! You have saved me!" He then began to cry again and thanked her repeatedly.

So this is how she concluded her story, adding with a smile, "This all happened some forty years ago, so you see Rabbi Biederman, I was an emissary of the Rebbe to Vienna many years before you arrived here."

Rabbi Biederman thanked her for her story, but was curious to know what was behind it. So he began to investigate, and discovered that Dr. Viktor Frankl had become a very famous psychologist, and was still alive! He was 87 years old at the time, and it turned out that he was a regular donor to the Chabad House in Vienna!

So Rabbi Biederman decided to call him up and to ask him if he remembered Margarete Chayos and the regards she had given him from Rabbi Schneerson some forty years ago.

Dr. Frankl responded, "I don't remember the name Margarete Chayos, but of course I remember that day! I will never forget it. My gratitude to Rabbi Schneerson is eternal."

Viktor Frankl's Search for Meaning

As a young man, Viktor Frankl excelled in the study of psychiatry at the University of Vienna, and had been in contact with Dr. Sigmund Freud and Dr. Alfred Adler, two of the founders of the psychoanalytic movement. After he graduated, he worked as a doctor in Vienna's General Hospital and the Rothschild Hospital. But when the Nazis came to power, he and his family were sent to the Theresienstadt concentration camp, where he tried to help other prisoners as a doctor and psychiatrist. But later, he was transferred to Auschwitz and Dachau, where he survived as a laborer before finally being liberated by American soldiers. Unfortunately, his parents had died in Auschwitz, and his pregnant wife had been murdered in Bergen-Belsen.

Despite all the tragedy he had seen, he had not become despondent. He had experienced moments in the midst of his suffering in the camps which told him that there is always something available to us which allows us to transcend our suffering—an act of kindness, or a value of deep personal meaning. And this insight propelled him to develop a therapeutic method radically different from that of Freud or the other psychiatric therapies of the time. He called it Logotherapy, from the Greek word, *logos,* 'meaning.'

Dr. Frankl said, "We who lived in concentration camps can remember the men who walked through the huts comforting others, giving away their last pieces of bread. They may have been few in number, but they offer sufficient proof that everything can be taken from a man but one thing—the last of the human freedoms—to choose one's attitude in any given set of circumstances, to choose one's own way."

Nevertheless, in the 1940's and 50's, Freud's ideas of psychoanalysis dominated the universities, and Frankl's ideas were dismissed as "unscientific" and even "fanatic religiosity." Thus, he told Rabbi Biederman:

"Rabbiner Biederman! I survived the German death camps and retained my spirit there but I could not survive the merciless derision and taunting of my colleagues undermining my every attempt at progress. Finally, after years of it, I was drained, exhausted, and depressed. I fell into a melancholy and decided to quit. I had no friends, no supporters, no pupils. I began drafting my resignation.

"And suddenly, in walks a woman who gives me regards from a Rabbi Schneerson from Brooklyn, New York! Hope! Inspiration! I could not believe my ears. Somebody in Brooklyn, no less a Chassidic Rebbe, knew about me! Appreciated me! He knew my predicament! He cared. At that time I was a nobody; rejected and alone! This was a miracle! How did he do these things?

"Indeed, his words came true. I fought! And shortly thereafter, I was given a Chair at the University. My book, *Man's Search for Meaning* was translated into English and suddenly I became one of the most celebrated psychiatrists of the generation."

Now Rabbi Biederman understood Dr. Frankl's emotional reaction to the Lubavitcher Rebbe's strange message. The meaning he had found in his life since the Holocaust had momentarily been eclipsed, when suddenly, the Rebbe's message burst into his life like a ray of sunlight, proving everything he had believed about Logotherapy![8]

Sparks of Wisdom

There are many activities available to us which might be called meaningful and we need to engage in as many of them as is possible. Some of these include time spent building our relationship with G-d, activities with family and friends, or time spent helping others. These things are deeply satisfying and touch us in a way that our less personal activities do not. Often we

---

[8] Retold from *Country Yossi Family Magazine*, 93-95.

encounter times when our lives seem to have become nothing but routine. We just go through the motions, mechanically, without any sense of interest or excitement. We search for what's missing but don't seem to find any enduring solutions. But if we would only get involved in a meaningful project this would ignite our spirits and provide us with a renewed passion and vitality.

Meaningful activities
Kindle the human spirit.

II

*"I know what happiness is,
for I have done good work."*
— Robert Louis Stevenson

The Mission

A large insurance company hired a research team to observe its claims processing clerks, and to assess the culture of the company as a whole.

One Friday afternoon, with twenty minutes still remaining on the shift, a researcher noticed that many clerks had actually stopped working, but still punched-out at five o'clock.

Later, the researcher had the opportunity to interview one of these clerks and said: "A couple of weeks ago, I noticed that you stopped working at twenty minutes to five, but didn't actually punch-out until five. Why was that?"

The clerk replied, "We have a policy that we can't leave until five."

The researcher tried again, "I mean, why did you stop working with twenty minutes left in the shift?"

The clerk shrugged her shoulders, "It was the weekend."

"Did you know that you still had six more insurance claims in your in-basket?"

The clerk answered, "They'd still be there Monday."

The researcher asked, "Do you know the company's mission statement?"

"Sure." Then she read from the framed poster on the wall, "Maximize the return on investment for shareowners."

Then the researcher asked a final question, "Does that inspire you to do a good job?"

The clerk looked at him with raised eyebrows, "Are you serious?"

Later that month, the researchers presented their findings to the companies executives. It turned out that the employees were basically satisfied with their pay, their benefits, and the way they were treated. But they had little or no sense of purpose or meaning in their work. And this often led to unproductive behaviors. So the researchers recommended that the company focus on a shared vision that would actually inspire the workers to invest in their work.

The executives responded that they already had a mission statement. So the researchers shared the response of the claims clerk who found the mission statement meaningless. And the executives 'got it.'

After that, they really began to look at their mission and its meaning: *Is it just the 'bottom line'? Or do we actually contribute something to society? Who benefits from our work? And is that important to us?*

One of the vice presidents began reading through old speeches given by past presidents to see if she could find any clues to the early leaders' vision for the company. And there she found a speech given by the founder in 1904, in which he stated: "The purpose for our enterprise is to reduce financial hardship and human suffering. And to the degree we do it well, we shall prosper."

Wow! Like everyone else, she mostly thought that the purpose of the company was "to invest premiums." It was a business after all. But now she began to think more about the company's responsibilities to its policyholders and employees, and also to society.

Thus, she and others began a process of re-writing the company's mission statement around the words of the founder in order to change the entire culture of the company. Moreover, she included the ordinary workers in the process as well.

Eighteen months later, the researchers were invited back to see if anything had changed. After they had finished their observation, one of the researchers again interviewed the claims clerk who had stopped working twenty minutes early in the previous analysis. This time he had noticed that she punched-out at five o'clock, returned to her desk, and worked another twenty-five minutes before going home!

So he said to her: "I noticed that you punched out at five, then worked an additional twenty five minutes before leaving. Why?"

She responded, "Well, we're having some overtime pressures, so they've asked us to punch out at five."

He rephrased his question, "What I mean is, why did you work another twenty-five minutes after punching-out?"

She said, "There were still seven claims in my in-basket."

"They'll still be there Monday," he suggested.

The clerk looked at him seriously and said, "You don't understand: Oklahoma recently had a terrible series of tornadoes, and those people really need their checks."

Then the researcher asked, "Do you know the company's mission?"

"Yes," she replied, and recited it without looking at the poster: " 'To reduce financial hardship and human suffering.' That's what my job's all about."[9]

Sparks of Wisdom

Our jobs have a great impact on our lives. We should view them not only as a means to make money, but also, as an opportunity to make the world a better place. When we treat our 'customers' with respect, honestly trying to fulfill their needs, we are actually bringing them a little bit of happiness. When we create good 'products,' we make the world run just a little better. If we view our jobs in this light, then they become truly meaningful.

Look at the ways in which your job helps people
And keep these in focus as you do your work.

---

[9] Retold from Kerry Patterson, Joseph Grenny, Al Switzler, and Ron Macmillan, *The Balancing Act: Mastering the Competing Demands of Leadership.*

III

"Money can be the husk of many things but not the kernel; it brings you food but not appetite, medicine but not health, acquaintances but not friends, service but not loyalty, days of joy, but not peace of happiness."

— Henrik Ibsen

Money or Meaning?

A young man came to Rabbi Abraham Twerski because he was experiencing a feeling of futility in his life. His father was very wealthy businessman, and consequently, the young man had every material thing he could desire. At one point, he said to Rabbi Twerski: "I think my father is crazy; he has more money than he could consume if he lived to be a thousand years old, but he still goes to the office every day to make more money. I already have all the money I can use. I have a condominium on the Riviera and another on the West Coast. I have a stable of horses. I have or can get everything a person could possibly want. I just don't have any taste for living. It is all meaningless. To tell the truth, I've often thought of suicide."

So Rabbi Twerski asked the young man why he did not use his money to provide for the needy; and he responded: "Give away my money? Why would I want to do that?"[10]

Sparks of Wisdom

Because all of his attention was given only to himself, he had lost all his taste for life. Some people believe that money will bring them happiness. But the evidence from various studies has shown that wealthy people are no happier than the average person. This is because happiness comes as a result of living a wholesome and meaningful life; and this is achieved by making the right choices in life, and cannot be bought with money. However, if money is used to support other people and meaningful projects, it can also become a source of joy.

Money cannot take the place of meaning.

---

[10] Retold from Abraham J. Twerski. *Visions of the Fathers,* 318-19.

The Art of Friendship

I

"The world will be a better place when the power of love replaces the love of power."

A Little Kindness . . .

Because of its rich Jewish history, Spain is a popular tourist destination for many Jews. Thus, Rabbi Yitzchok Goldstein, a Chabad rabbi in Madrid, often finds himself acting as an unofficial guide for those Jews who have come to visit the ancient synagogue in which he prays. As such, he has also instructed his children to make all the tourists feel welcome and comfortable in the synagogue, even helping them to recite the prayers on occasion.

One day, an unfamiliar man entered the synagogue, and seeing him, Rabbi Goldstein's son immediately went over to welcome him, as he had been taught. When he discovered that the man was unfamiliar with the prayers, he stayed close and helped him with them.

This man soon became a regular at the synagogue, and over time, very friendly with

Rabbi Goldstein and his family.

One day, after he had known him for a while, the man turned to Rabbi Goldstein and said—"I have something that I feel I should share with you about my first visit to the synagogue. At the time, my life had become unbearable, and I was seriously considering suicide. So I went to the roof of a tall building and was about to jump when, strangely enough, it occurred to me that I should probably say 'goodbye' to G-d first. Since I am Jewish, I decided that the most appropriate place to do that would be at a synagogue.

"As soon as I arrived, I was greeted by your son, who was so kind, and took such a genuine interest in me throughout the prayers, that by the time I walked out of the synagogue, I felt a renewed will to live, and decided right then and there that I would not commit suicide! Instead, I decided to begin rebuilding my life."[11]

The Power of Friendship

Back when there were no public water-lines supplying fresh water to every home, people used to have to hire 'water carriers' to bring

---

[11] I first saw this story in the magazine, *Beis Moshiach*, and was so inspired that I contacted Rabbi Goldstein and asked him if it actually happened—It had! I have re-told it from the magazine version and as I heard it from Rabbi Goldstein.

the water in buckets directly to their homes each day from the well or river. On one particularly hot day, a local water carrier was walking along the road, toiling under his heavy load—two full buckets of water suspended on either end of a shaft laid across his shoulders—and feeling very depressed.

He kept thinking about how hot it was, how overwhelmed he felt just then, and how his body seemed to be getting weaker and weaker every day. How could he possibly go on? Just then, he met a good friend of his, and put down his buckets to spend a few minutes chatting with his friend. After an enjoyable conversation, he felt refreshed and took up his load with a new vigor. It was the same load, and the sun was still hot, but somehow he felt renewed, and now went about his work with a smile and pleasant melody on his lips.[12]

Sparks of Wisdom

In our daily lives, we come into contact with so many people. Sometimes that person whom we merely 'bump into' becomes an important friend as we discover how much we have in common, or how similar our personalities are.

---

[12] Based on a parable in the *Likkutei Torah* or *Torah Or* of the Alter Rebbe, Rabbi Shneur Zalman of Liadi.

On the other hand, some friendships take a little more time and effort. Maybe we don't have so much in common; maybe we are even quite different. But when we give these people 'a chance,' taking the time to learn something about them and their lives, we can sometimes form friendships that are even stronger than the ones we have with those who are so much more like ourselves. All it takes is a little kindness, and a willingness to be open to new people and new experiences.

Few things in life are as powerful for promoting well-being and happiness as kindness and friendship; these two things make us (and those around us) stronger and more content, and not least important, bring excitement and new vitality into our lives.

Make acts of kindness and friendship
A part of every day.

II

*"The only way to have a friend
is to be one"*
— Ralph Waldo Emerson

You Get What You Give

One day, a little boy became angry with his mother because she had reprimanded him. So, in order to vent his feelings of anger, he ran to the edge of the ravine just outside of his house and shouted as loud as he could—"I hate you! I hate you! I hate you!"

Then, almost immediately, he heard an angry, hollow sounding voice, rumbling back at him—"I hate you! I hate you! I hate you!"

The boy was terrified and ran back to his mother crying, "Mama, there is a mean man in the ravine who says he hates me!"

So the mother took the boy by the hand and led him back to the ravine. Then, in a tender and pleasant voice, she called out—"I love you! I love you! I love you!"

> A sweet sonorous voice echoed back, kind happy voice echoed back—"I love you! I love you! I love you!"[13]

The Fountain of Youth?

Back in the 1950's, researchers found that the citizens of Rosetta, Pennsylvania, were living longer lives than people in any other part of the country. So the government funded a study which sought to identify a possible explanation for this phenomenon.

When the research was complete, they found that the city of Rosetta had an exceptionally strong sense of 'community.' Its people were very close to each other, and lived tightly knit lives, centered to a large extent around group activities with friends and family. Moreover, the houses in this city were built with large front porches on which people tended to sit, talking with their neighbors late into the night.

Thirty years later, a new group of researchers found that the lifespan in Rosetta had since declined, and was now similar to the rest of the country. They found that the children of the former residents did not have the same sense community as their parents.

---

[13] Retold from Morris Mandel, *Stories to Live By*.

> Also, the newer houses in which they lived were being built without porches, so people were now living more isolated lives.[14]

Sparks of Wisdom

We all value friends, but not all of us find it easy to make friends, or have as many friends as we would like. So how should we go about making more friends? Well, most of us pursue relationships with people whom we either like or respect. But this method of making friends limits our field of potential friends considerably. If we would have more friends, we might consider the advice implicit in the book of Proverbs (27:19), where we are told that the human heart mirrors other hearts. That is to say, the way you feel toward someone else is the way they will feel toward you, since the human heart picks up and reflects the feelings of its neighbor and responds with similar feelings. So if I like someone, it is fairly natural for that person to like me; and if I dislike them, then it is also quite natural for them to dislike me. Thus, if you become a person who likes people, they will naturally respond with the similar feelings toward you.

Now, you might say, "What do you mean? I like people!" But what most of us mean by that is that we like *some* people. Here we are talking about, liking people generally. Perhaps the most

---

[14] Retold from a talk by David Pelcovitz given at the International Conference of Shluchos in Brooklyn, New York.

important step in becoming a person that likes people is to adopt an attitude of love and friendship towards *all* people.

Friendship is the great art of the human spirit.

III

Two are better than one …
for should they fall,
one can raise the other;
but woe to him who is alone
when he falls,
for there is no one to raise him.
— Ecclesiastes 4:9-10

What is a Friend?

A newspaper once offered a prize for the best definition of 'a friend.' These are just a few of the thousands of definitions that flooded in:

"A friend is one who understands our silence."

"A friend is a watch that beats true for all time and never runs down."

"A friend is one who multiplies joys, divides grief, and whose honesty is inviolable."

> This, however, is the definition that finally won the prize:
>
> *"A friend is one who comes in when the whole world has gone out."*[15]

Sparks of Wisdom

There is an unusual Jewish teaching that says, "Buy yourself a friend." Is that right? Shouldn't a friendship be built on genuine feelings of love and respect? After all, what good is a friendship that has to be bought?

In Hebrew, the word for 'friend' is *chaver*, which also means 'to connect.' For when two people make a connection and come together as a unit they can be called friends. Now, the bonding of two people can happen in many different ways. As we said earlier, some people are simply similar in nature and bond very quickly, while others may need to spend a lot of time together before a bond is formed. However, this teaching tells us that human nature responds most profoundly to the situation in which another person 'comes through' for us, or helps us in some manner.

Of course, for a friendship to be truly successful, there needs to be respect, trust, and love. Nevertheless, it is a good idea for us to be giving in our relationships, and thereby plant the seeds for the strongest possible friendships.

---
[15] Retold from Morris Mandel's column, "Youth Speaks Up" in the *Jewish Press*.

*Helping a friend
Is an opportunity for deeper friendship.*

The Art of Marriage

I

"Therefore, a man shall leave his father and mother and cleave unto his wife."
— Genesis 2:24

Real Love

Once, a young woman came to see the Rebbe[16] to discuss some prospective matches that had been suggested to her, and why none of the young men appealed to her. The Rebbe smiled at her and said, "You have read too many romance novels. Love is not the overwhelming, blinding emotion you find in the world of fiction. Real love is an emotion that intensifies throughout life. It is the small, everyday acts of being together that make love flourish. It is sharing and caring and respecting one another. It is building a life together, a family and a home. As two lives unite to form one, over time there is a point where each partner feels a part of the other, where each

---

[16] Rabbi Menachem Mendel Schneerson (1902-1994), the 7th Lubavitcher Rebbe, one of the greatest spiritual leaders of the 20th century.

partner can no longer visualize life without the other at his or her side."[17]

Sparks of Wisdom

In the Bible, we are told that G-d first created the human being and then removed one of its "sides" which was fashioned into woman. G-d then brought this newly fashioned woman to marry the man that was left behind. Thus we see that man and woman—originally one being—each hold the missing part of the other and only become complete again in marriage.

Before we get married, we often have a feeling of anxiety, which is the result of our missing a part of our own essence. But when we get married, we begin to feel whole again.

The intimacy of marriage
Is greater than any other intimacy,
Since marriage is the re-union
Of two parts of the same whole.

---

[17] Retold from Simon Jacobson, *Towards a Meaningful Life*, 57. Nevertheless, the Rebbe is quoted verbatim.

II

*"Love is not what conquers the heart,
but that which is conquered
by the heart."*

The Gift

Douglas was a young writer who told Rebbetzin Esther Jungreis he was writing a book about marriage and that he had interviewed his grandparents about it.

"Why your grandparents?" She asked.

He answered, "To my mind, they are the perfect couple, totally happy with each other. As a matter of fact, I don't think I've ever seen them fight, and believe me, Rebbetzin, I've observed the grandparents of many of my friends: they can really be difficult, arguing over all kinds of nonsense. So I figured that my grandparents would be a good story."

So she asked him to tell her about them.

"Well," he said, "I decided to speak to them individually, and what an experience that was!

First, I asked Grandma how it was that I never saw her fight with Grandpa.

" 'What's there to fight about?' she said. 'I'm happy if he's happy.' And as a case in point, she told me that when they fly she would much prefer to have the window seat, but she knows that grandpa likes it, 'so I let him have it. No big deal. Like I said, I'm happy if he's happy.'

"Now what was remarkable about this conversation," Douglas continued, "was that later, when I interviewed Grandpa, he cited the same example. 'I know that your grandmother likes the aisle seat on the plane, so I always let her have it, even though I prefer it.'

"To be honest with you," Douglas told her, "at first I thought that was real dumb. All those years sitting in seats they didn't want thinking they were pleasing the other! That could never happen to someone of my generation. We would just say outright, 'I want the aisle seat' or 'I want the window seat,' and we would expect to be accommodated. But Grandma and Grandpa have only one agenda—making each other happy—and that's kind of touching, don't you think?"

Rebbetzin Esther said she did, but had to ask, "Did you ever enlighten them about their misunderstanding?"

Douglas answered, "I almost did, but then I realized that that would be cruel. For the past forty years they've been going down to Florida, and every time they got on a plane, they thought they were giving each other a gift. I wouldn't want to spoil that. That's what makes their love so special."[18]

One More Thing

Although not a doctor himself, Dr. Abraham Twerski's father knew a lot about medicine. As a rabbi, he made daily visits to patients in the hospital, and after years of discussing their cases with the doctors, he had acquired a pretty fair knowledge of the medical field. So when he developed cancer of the pancreas, involving the liver, he said to his son, "Chemotherapy doesn't do anything for pancreatic cancer does it?"

His son replied that it did not.

"Then there is no point in suffering all the side effects of chemotherapy if it cannot do any good, is there?"

His son agreed that he was right, and concurred with his decision not to have chemotherapy.

---

[18] Retold from Rebbetzin Esther Jungreis, *The Committed Marriage*, 96-98. Quotes verbatim.

Nevertheless, his father's doctor told his mother, "There's not much we can do for the rabbi. At best, chemotherapy can get us three more months."

So his mother told his father, "Three months? Why, it would be worth it for even three days! Every single day is precious!" She insisted that he undergo chemotherapy.

After his mother left the room, the rabbi said to his son, "I'm sorry that the doctor gave Mother the wrong information. I know that it will not extend my life for three months. But if I refuse chemotherapy, then when I die, Mother will say, 'Why didn't I insist on it? If I had insisted on it, he would still be alive,' and she will feel guilty for not insisting. I don't want her to feel guilty. So I will take chemotherapy."

Then his father paused and added, "I've done many things for Mother during our fifty-two years. This gives me a chance to do one last thing."[19]

Sparks of Wisdom

The word 'love' can mean many things: when I say, "I love ice cream," I do not mean that I

---

[19] Retold from Abraham J. Twerski, *Happiness and the Human Spirit: The Spirituality of Becoming the Best You Can Be*, 77-78. Quotes verbatim.

actually love the product—ice cream—but rather that I love the taste and experience of eating ice cream; however, when I say, "I love my child," I mean that I love the person, my child. In the one, my love is self-focused, focused on my own experience, and in the other, my love is focused on another.

The love of marriage actually has both meanings: when I say, "I love my wife," I mean that I love the feeling and experience of sharing my life with my wife; on the other hand, I also love the person, my wife. A marriage cannot survive when the love is self-focused on one's own feelings and desires; for these are unstable and subject to change—sometimes strong and sometimes weak. So there also needs to be another love which is other focused.

The way to ensure that your marriage is something more than self-focused is to be very caring to your spouse; for the very act of taking care of another shifts the focus away from ourselves, thus strengthening the other important dimension of marital love.

Give back to your spouse, unselfishly,
For this is the other half of love.

III

"To give is to live."
— Morris Mandel

Giving What You Want to Get

Leora said to her marriage counselor, "He simply doesn't love me anymore; maybe he never really did." Surprisingly, in response, her marriage counselor gave her a list of ten things to do for him every day!

"What?" said Leora, balking at the list, "I'm supposed to do all this for him when he doesn't even love me anymore?"

But her counselor only said: "Give it a try and see what happens. Come back next week and we'll talk about it."

The next week, Leora returned very excited—"I don't know what happened," she said, "he's so much nicer to me now. I guess I was wrong; my husband really does love me after all![20]

---

[20] Retold from Yirmiyohu Abramov, and Tehilla Abramov, *Two Halves of a Whole*, Southfield, Michigan, Targum Press, 1994.

Sparks of Wisdom

As we said before about "other focused love," if you want to have a successful marriage, it is necessary to be committed to fulfilling the wishes of your spouse. This commitment is the oil that keeps the love of marriage burning brightly. Closeness and commitment are really inseparable. If someone finds themselves slipping in their commitment to their spouse, they will surely find themselves losing the closeness as well. Many marriages fall apart as time passes because one partner or both lose the connection and commitment to the other's needs.

In order for marriage to succeed,
There needs to be commitment to the other's needs.

The Art of Thinking

I

"Some of the best things to lay up for a rainy day are your worries."
— Morris Mandel

Controlling Thoughts

A man came to the Maggid of Mezritch with a problem. He said: "My mind is always straying during prayer; I am constantly being distracted by my thoughts!"

The Maggid said: "I think you should go and see my disciple, Rabbi Ze'ev of Zhitomer. He will help you with this problem."

So the man traveled to Zhitomer to see Rabbi Ze'ev and arrived after nightfall. With some difficulty, he found Rabbi Ze'ev's house in the darkness and knocked loudly on the door, anxious to come in out of the cold. But there was no answer. He knocked again—still no answer. Now, he was getting upset and knocked still louder. Nothing.

He was forced to spend the night outside.

In the morning, Rabbi Ze'ev opened the door and welcomed him warmly. The man told him why he had come and Rabbi Ze'ev invited him to stay in his home during his visit. He was surprised by this warm reception after being ignored the night before, but decided it would be disrespectful to mention it to the rabbi.

He stayed with Rabbi Ze'ev for several days and learned much from him, but not once had the rabbi so much as mentioned the question he had come to have answered. So, finally, he broached the subject with Rabbi Ze'ev: "Rabbi, why won't you teach me how to control my thoughts? After all, this is why the Maggid, your teacher, sent me to you."

Rabbi Ze'ev answered, "Because I already have."

"When?" the man asked.

"On the night you first arrived. You knocked and knocked on my door, wanting to come in. I knew you were there, of course, but I decided not to let you enter. No matter how hard you knocked, I had no intention of letting you in. That is also the secret of controlling your thoughts."[21]

---

[21] Retold from Shloma Majeski, *The Chassidic Approach to Joy*, 50-51.

Sparks of Wisdom

Some people believe that the difference between a 'good life' and a 'bad life' has to do with external circumstances: how much money you have, how many comforts, or what kind of a job you have. But the truth is, what we choose to think about also has a strong effect on the quality of our lives. For instance, the *way* we think directly affects the way we feel. When we think about pleasant things, it raises our spirits and we feel good. When we think about negative things, it dampens our spirits and causes us stress. At times, we all have to think about negative things, but it is important to find the proper balance of thoughts. But sometimes we simply have to close the door on our negative thoughts and refuse to open it.

The way in which you choose to think
Can have a big influence on your quality of life.

II

"The pleasantest things in the world are pleasant thoughts; and the great art in life is to have as many of them as possible."
— Morris Mandel

Better Thoughts

Rabbi Dovid Goldwasser used to wonder whether or not he should leave the ringer on full or lower it before going to bed at night. After all, no one wants to be awakened in the middle of the night by a wrong number. Nevertheless, he kept it up "just in case." Thus, he was jarred out of a sound sleep at 3:00 in the morning by the sound of his phone ringing.

He answered the phone and a gruff voice on the other end said, "Hello, is this Rabbi Dovid Goldwasser?"

"Yes, this is he."

"Rabbi, I'm Officer Costanza of the NYPD. I've got a young lady here who is standing on the roof of her apartment building, ready to jump. She says you're her Rabbi, so maybe you could talk to her. She's serious, rabbi. She won't let us come within two feet of her, and she looks like the real thing. She just wants to speak to your first. Her name is Elaine Smith."

Rabbi Goldwasser had never received a phone call like this before. He tried to clear his head and prayed that he would be up to the challenge. But before he could even tell the officer that he didn't recognize the woman's name, the officer put her on the phone!

She spoke to him in a slow monotone, saying: "I can't go on anymore. I just want to end it all. The difficulties I've been having . . . they're just too much to bear. I can't take it any longer. I just want it to end. The pain I'm in. Going to school didn't help my existence—it's too painful. I'm alone. Don't you see that? I've tried to help myself, but I just can't seem to do it. I just can't. Nobody understands me. I want to put an end to this misery."

She continued in this way for a long time, while Rabbi Goldwasser paced back and forth in his bedroom with the phone pressed hard to his ear. He was both sweating and shivering—a human life hung in the balance! She needed a reason to go on; could he give her that reason? The only thing keeping her from a thirty-story descent at the moment was a telephone!

Finally, she paused, and the rabbi seized the moment: "Elaine, don't ever give up! A human being doesn't give up. Our Rabbis said that as long as a person lives there is hope. You have not exhausted every possibility of hope. You are young and you have many years ahead of you—happy years, fruitful years. Don't let this moment of desperation cloud everything you've accomplished in your life so far..."

She shouted back at him in bitterness, "That's not true! I haven't accomplished anything. I'm not a good person. I don't deserve to live." Then she said quietly, with a stifled sob, "Help me! I'm in pain."

He could tell from her voice that she was becoming more desperate by the minute. His mind raced for something to say that would turn her away from this course. Suddenly, he remembered meeting her at a symposium for Jewish professionals in upper Manhattan. He had delivered a lecture there about four years before, and remembered that she had mentioned her parents. So quickly he asked (in as casual a way as possible), "Elaine, how are your parents?"

To his horror, she started yelling: "Why do you ask me about my parents?! What do they have to do with this?! Why did you mention them?!"

He tried to calm her down: "Elaine, I only wanted to ask how your family was doing. Your parents have nothing to do with this. You're absolutely right. I only . . ."

She interrupted him, "Why aren't you here?"

"Give me fifteen minutes," he said, "and I'll be there."

She screamed, "No! Don't go! Don't hang up. Don't get off this phone."

Then she began rambling as before, and ended again with, "Why aren't you here?"

He offered to be there in fifteen minutes again, but she quickly said: "That's it! I'm, going to end it. I've had enough of this talk."

She sounded sincere, and he desperately searched for something to say. Should he risk reminding her about how she would be hurting her parents? No. Obviously that was a sore subject. Should he quote Jewish Sages about the sacredness of a human life?

His mind raced even as he tried to seem calm. Finally, he said: "Elaine, I accept your decision. But I still have one question I would like to ask you: what shall I tell your fiancée?"

Absolute silence followed. Then Elaine said in a subdued voice, "I don't have a fiancée."

"That's not true!" he said. "Forty days before a baby is formed, a Heavenly voice proclaims: 'The daughter of *this person* will marry *that person*.' Every soul that comes to this world has a soul partner somewhere. So that means that there is a soul partner waiting for you, too. And I just want to know what to tell him in case he asks me about you."

"You think I might one day stand under a Marriage canopy?"

"Elaine, I honestly believe so."

She started to sob, and moments later Rabbi Goldwasser heard a lot of shuffling sounds. A moment later, the police officer spoke into the phone with an undercurrent of strong emotion: "Okay, rabbi, we've got her. She's fine. We've got her. You did a good job, rabbi, and G-d bless you."

Rabbi Goldwasser felt drained and euphoric at the same time. He had already been blessed by G-d. G-d had given him the wisdom to give Elaine hope for the future. The pleasant thought that Elaine had of one day standing under the marriage canopy gave her the strength to make the decision to live on.[22]

Sparks of Wisdom

There are certain types of things that we think about that, generally speaking, are damaging to ourselves because they bring us a lot of stress. These are thoughts of hatred toward other people, self-loathing, jealously, and excessive worrying or fear.

Sometimes people feel there is nothing that they can do about such thoughts, since usually we don't consciously decide to think about those things. They just seem to infiltrate our minds on their own. However, while it is true that we don't have total control of what thoughts enter our mind, we can choose to discontinue thinking them. The human mind can only think effectively about one thing at a time. So if when a negative thought enters our mind, we consciously start to think about something else, we can force the negative thought out of our mind.

At times, negative thoughts can be very powerful. This is the case, for example, when we are very worried about something and it continues to invade our mind. At these times, we must be very strong and continue to battle the thought. Just as our muscles are strengthened by exercise and atrophy if we don't exercise them, a

---

[22] Retold (with quotes) from Dovid Goldwasser, *It Happened in Heaven*, 66-69.

negative thought is strengthened by continual thinking and weakens if we cease giving it our time and attention. When we do not allow ourselves to continue thinking the negative thought, we diminish the probability of its surfacing in the near future. Of course, it is possible that the thought will recur again, perhaps recur many times; but each time it is ignored, its power over you is weakened.

It is important to note that at times it is beneficial to continue thinking about something negative in order to deal with the situation responsibly, or to relieve some of the pain and tension that the situation might be bringing. Good judgment must be used in each situation to find the proper balance.

Controlling your thoughts is challenging

But always possible.

III

"Hanging on to resentment is allowing someone you dislike to live inside your head without paying you rent."
— Morris Mandel

The Prize

Once, there was a wealthy man who made a lavish party for his friends. He invited them to swim in his pool, which had sharks in it, and announced that whoever swam a lap and survived would get $100,000, a new car, and a new house.

After he said this, it was completely silent; it seemed that no one was willing to risk their life. All of a sudden, a splash was heard. Jack the tailor was in the pool! To everyone's surprise, he fought magnificently, thwarted the sharks, and despite many close calls, made it out of the pool alive! As he climbed out, he saw that everyone was stunned.

The wealthy man walked over to Jack, who barely had the strength to move, and said: "Congratulations, Jack! I am a man of my word. Next week you will receive a check in the mail, the deed to your new home, and a new Jaguar."

Breathless, Jack replied angrily: "My friend . . . I don't want your money . . . your house . . . or your car. All I want to know is who pushed me into the water!"[23]

Sparks of Wisdom

It's interesting that the man in the story is so angry and determined to know who pushed him in the pool that he cares nothing about the money, the house, or the car. While this is obviously just an amusing story, the truth is that we often act in the same fashion. Many times, when people hurt us, we carry the anger around in our hearts so long that we become oblivious to the fact that we are hurting ourselves with it and are missing out on the best of what life has to offer.

There is a saying, "The heaviest thing to carry is a grudge." How true! Grudges and anger eat us up on the inside and cause us a great deal of anguish. If we feel anger toward another person, we should take steps to minimize that anger before we end up missing out on the best of life.

When we carry hate in our hearts
We end up hurting ourselves.

---
[23] Heard from my friend, Yitzchok Abramowitz.

IV

*"To forgive is to emulate G-d,
To harbor resentment is to be
A prisoner of your own hate."*
— Rebbetzin Esther Jungreis

Freeing the Captive

Kalman was a 38-year-old man who consulted a therapist because he felt his life was falling apart. "I am extremely irritable," he told the therapist. "I have lower back pain and get these pounding headaches. As a result, I am continually depressed and nervous. My wife is a good woman, but still I shout at her for no reason. I don't know how long she is going to put up with me. I have no patience with my children either and yell at them too. I can't sleep, so I saw a psychiatrist who prescribed anti-depressants and tranquilizers for me. I have also seen two psychologists and they have not helped me.

"I know what my problem is," Kalman said. "I just don't know how to get over it. My father was a cruel man, and all I can remember about him is his screaming at me and insulting me. I wanted to run away from home many times because of it. Even after I grew up and married, he continued to harass me. And each time he calls, all my resentment toward him is refueled.

"This resentment is eating me up. Sometimes I have nightmares about his abusive behavior and it haunts me. I just don't know what to do about it."

The therapist considered a moment and said, "Have you thought of forgiving your father?"

Kalman looked like he had been hit by a truck. "Forgive him!?" He said. "Why should I forgive him? He should apologize to me! I don't want to forgive him; I don't even want anything to do with him!"

The therapist said: "Forgiving him doesn't necessarily mean that you must have a relationship with him, but it may help you to rid yourself of your anger, the anger that is causing you to be irritable with your own family."

Kalman asked, "So what if I say I forgive him? How will that change things between us?"

"Saying you forgive him will not do anything for your relationship with him. But

> hanging on to your anger is not hurting him; *it is hurting you*. Forgiveness is a long process, but if you're willing to work at it, I'll be glad to help you."[24]

Sparks of Wisdom

People often say things like: "Why should I forgive? They don't deserve my forgiveness; they haven't even had the decency to say they're sorry!" But we don't only forgive people because they deserve it; we also forgive them for the sake of our own well-being and peace of mind.

It's a sad reality that when someone hurts us, we tend to pass that hurt on. If the hurt was intense or frequent, we have a hard time ridding ourselves of it. Even if we decide not to think about these experiences, the remembrance, the resentment and the anger over these experiences invades our thoughts at unexpected moments and conditions the way we feel and react to things.

Psychologists believe that resentment is extremely damaging to us and can inhibit the amount of joy we experience in our personal lives. So how can we remove the resentment and hurt from our hearts and minds? *Through forgiveness.* When you truly forgive someone, you drain the poison of anger, resentment and negativity from your system.

---

[24] Retold from Abraham J. Twerski, *Forgiveness: Don't Let Resentment Keep You Captive,* 18-21.

*Through forgiveness, you can rid yourself
Of your resentment and anger.*

V

"Behave as if you are happy and the happiness will follow."
— Rabbi Nachman of Bratzlav

The Miracle of Laughter

A cardiologist in Mumbai, India, Dr. Madan Kataria, researched the effects of laughter on the body, and found to his surprise that laughter lowered stress-levels, led to better breathing, and heightened immune response—regardless of whether the laughter was genuine or not! Thus, Dr. Kataria decided to create laughter exercises in order to produce health-inducing effects. In time, he took his exercises into the world, organizing laughter clubs in Indian public parks. The idea soon caught on and today there are an estimated 8,000 laughter clubs in the world.

In a typical laughter club, the instructor might tell everyone to put on laugher cream or brush their teeth with laughter paste and then tell everyone to look at their neighbor and start laughing: "Ho-ho-ho Ha-ha-ha!" Before long, the atmosphere gets so silly that the laughter becomes real laughter!

> Today, the idea has even spread to businesses in India who now require their workers to begin each day with laughter exercises, citing its positive effects on the workers attitudes and alertness![25]

Sparks of Wisdom

It's ironic that, although we all strive for happiness in our lives, we so rarely try to do anything about it when we are feeling down. It is simply hard for us to be positive when we are feeling negative. Nevertheless, if we would only make the effort to think and act positively, perhaps even to laugh, we would find that we would start feeling better immediately.

There is a Jewish teaching, "The heart follows our actions." This means that the way we act will ultimately awaken corresponding feelings in our heart. Therefore, it is very important to have a joyous disposition.

Here are some suggestions: sing an upbeat song, make a joke and smile, talk about positive things, and most importantly, focus your attention on the positive.

Even when you are down, behave joyously,
And watch the wonders it will create.

---

[25] Retold from Eliyahu Paley, *Mishpacha Magazine*, 22.

The Art of Attitude

I

"The wise man doesn't expect to find life worth living, he makes it that way."
— Ancient Greek Proverb

A Beautiful Year

"It is going to be a beautiful year," the little girl exclaimed as she put her new calendar on the wall.

Hearing this, her friend asked, "How do you know? A year is a long time, and you never know what's going to happen."

The girl answered, "Yes, but a day isn't a long time; I'm going to take it one day at a time and *make it beautiful*. I'm gonna' make sure that every day gets something beautiful into it!"[26]

Sparks of Wisdom

"One man gets nothing but discord from the keys of a piano, another gets harmony. No one claims the piano is at fault. Life is that same way. The discord is there; so is the harmony. Play it

---
[26] Retold from Morris Mandel, *Stories to Live By*.

correctly and it gives forth the beauty; play it falsely and it will utter ugliness. But life is not at fault. The trouble lies in the player."[27]

With effort and creativity,
You can make your life unique.

---

[27] A well-known, though unattributed quote.

II

"A pessimist sees the difficulty in the opportunity; an optimist sees the opportunity in every difficulty."
— Winston Churchill

Good Fortune

Dear Beth—

I have just read your letter and I feel that I must respond!!! I would like to tell you some of my life story and my experiences with good fortune.

I am the child of a Jewish couple who did not want children. Never in my life have I ever been told that I am loved or wanted and worse was the horrific, verbal and physical abuse that I suffered over the years from my father. As soon as I finished school, I ran away from home. I want you to know that I had no help or assistance as I got a lowly job and put myself through college, qualifying with distinction, and supported myself. I paid for my own rent, food and clothing (which came from second-hand shops). The hardships I experienced during this period are too numerous to mention, and I leave them to your imagination. But, despite everything, today, thank G-d, I have a loving close relationship with my children and have brought them up in a secure, happy home. I did not allow my past to destroy my life. If anything, my parents were an opportunity for me to learn how *not* to be a parent, how to treat children with respect, to teach me that words hurt worse than fists.

I also learned that if you want something to happen, you have to do it for yourself. You can sit and pray and pray all day, every day, but nothing is going to happen if you don't open yourself up to seeing the opportunities presented to you and make it happen! Believe me when I say that everything was against me! But if you work with G-d to make things happen, they will. Throughout this time, I prayed to *G-d* to give me strength, but I did not pray for unrealistic things such as getting my parent to love me or for me to win a jackpot to pay for my college fees. My future was in my hands and I understood that.

My first child was born with two birth defects; I nearly lost my second child and then, many years later, lost a much-wanted baby. Although I have found this hard to deal with, I have seized the opportunity to learn from this experience. I believe that when life trips you up, you have to pick up the pieces. I have learned how people feel in this situation. I have learned that people need love and support and definitely, not all sorts of questions about the gory details.

My oldest child is one of my heroes because she had challenges and she decided to make her own future, and not the one predicted by doctors. My gorgeous daughter was told that she would never be able to run, and today, with her incredible determination, strength and faith in G-d, and herself, she made it happen. When she ran at her school's one-mile race, you can imagine my shock, surprise and joy at seeing my daughter coming in second! She could have chosen to have no *good fortune* and not to be gifted, but she chose to do it, to make it happen—yes, she made her own good fortune.

My grandmother, whom I adored, got sick, and nobody in my family was interested in this frail old woman, especially when she was in a coma in the last eight months of her life. I visited her daily even when she could not "give" me anything or respond to me. She died one evening with me at her side telling her how much I loved and adored her. I was heartbroken beyond words. My grandmother was an opportunity to learn about love that one can give unconditionally. I learned about people's need for dignity and love when their bodies fail, and the need for company and love when you know that you have nothing to give in return. I am so grateful to *G-d* for having given me the opportunity to have had my grandmother, to have had the privilege of being with her on her final journey to the world to come. People change when they are sick and elderly and need to feel secure and loved.

I'm sorry that your mother has undergone a personality change, but please be patient and give her the security and sensitivity she needs. You have a challenge here to give back to your mother the security and respect she gave you. How fortunate you are to have this opportunity to give and sad that your siblings missed out.

You missed out on a lesson on how to create good fortune because you had to attend to your mother. Personally, I think that G-d was teaching you something right then and there. The lesson is that your first priority is to honor and respect your mother and help her through this frightening time, and I firmly believe that the more one gives to others and does acts of kindness, the more one will be blessed with good fortune. Why did you presume that a class on creating good fortune was on how to create good fortune only for yourself? Well, instead, G-d gave you the opportunity to give good fortune to someone else who needed it!

I married a man of comfortable means, and a few months after my second child was born, his business was liquidated and we lost everything. I couldn't even put food on the table. For four years, after this, I was the sole support while my husband paid off other debts and I worked at three jobs. I remember this period in a blur of exhaustion. This was an opportunity for my husband to know that I loved and adored him enormously and to prove that I am here for the good as well as the bad times. I cannot explain what this has done for my marriage. At times, it was difficult while I was sometimes so angry with him for getting us into this situation, but I chose to focus on all his good, and when he felt like a loser, I made sure that I and the children treated him like a king. My husband had to start from scratch again and also learn from the opportunity given to him. He has picked himself up and today is the head of a huge business and we are financially successful. My husband today is so proud of me and so grateful for helping him see the opportunities provided by what happened and the biggest thing he learned is that good fortune can happen only when you make it happen!

Am I also good fortune-less? The answer is absolutely NO!! Did G-d abandon and punish me or not hear my prayers? Absolutely NOT!! I want you to know that throughout this journey

I believed in *G-d* and have known that these things didn't happen to me because I was good fortune-less. Please know that G-d does hear your prayer, but He needs you to be partners with Him to make things happen.

Reading over what I have written, I apologize if I have made everything sound too easy or if I sound arrogant. I don't mean to be. I am sharing my very private journey with you in the hope that you will see that you are special and beautiful in ways that you haven't been able to see and that you can change things, and you are definitely not someone who isn't gifted. If you were given this label, you may see things as affirmations that it was true—but it isn't! We all have our challenges and mine was to help achieve what I needed to achieve. I pray that you will see the opportunities in yours and that you will have the strength, faith and motivation to do so. I hope that you will see the opportunities presented to you to make *good fortune* for others and to make *good fortune* for yourself.

I would like to end off with a little story I heard from Rebbetzin Jungreis when she spoke to our community that has always stuck in my mind. When Rebbetzin Jungreis was in Bergen Belsen concentration camp, her father, Rabbi Avraham Halevi Jungreis, told her and her brothers that there, in the camps, they had an opportunity to help others: that by smiling, they could give hope to those who felt hopeless and strength to those who could no longer go on. When children smile, they give adults hope, strength and courage. The Rebbetzin's father taught his children a priceless lesson—even when there was nothing to give, they could still uplift others with a smile and make a difference in their lives. The Rebbetzin and her brothers could have chosen to think how *good fortune-less* they were, but instead, they seized the moment and chose to give others a smile, new life and hope, and that's the true meaning of *good fortune.*[28]

The Jewel in the Crown

There once was a king whose crown had a magnificent jewel in its center. But one day, when the crown was being polished, it was dropped and the jewel was scratched. So the king called the royal jewelers to see if it might be fixed, but none of them was able to fix the jewel. At last, a humble jeweler came and said that he could fix the jewel. He immediately set to work etching a pattern of branches around the scratch until it was transformed into a beautiful tree. This tree made the jewel even

---

[28] From "Rebbetzin's Viewpoint," Rebbetzin Esther Jungreis, reprinted by special arrangement with *The Jewish Press.*

more unique and beautiful than it had been before, and the crown became famous as a work of art.[29]

Sparks of Wisdom

When people experience difficulties, they often say, "Why me?" meaning, "Why was I singled out for this hardship?" But we can ask the same question in a different way, "Why me?" meaning, "What am I supposed to learn from this experience?" Judaism teaches us that there are no accidents, that G-d runs the world with purpose and reason. If we encounter a difficult life experience, we should try to find a hidden good in the experience. At times, it might be difficult to find good in a situation, but we can still hold on to the belief that something good will be born from the experience.

There is a secret blessing in every experience.

---

[29] Retold from a version by David Pelcovitz, given during an interview with *Mishpacha Magazine*.

III

"Life is like a blanket too short. You pull it up and your toes rebel, you yank it down and shivers meander about your shoulder; but cheerful folks manage to draw their knees up and pass a very comfortable night."
— Marion Howard

Thank You

When Joseph Cabiliv awoke in the Rambam hospital in Haifa, he had no idea how he had gotten there. What he did know is that he felt excruciating pain in his legs. So, with some trepidation, he lifted the sheet and saw to his horror that both legs had been amputated!

The day before, he had been on reserve duty in the Israeli Defense Force patrolling the Golan Heights with several other soldiers. Suddenly, their Jeep hit an old Syrian land mine and two of his comrades were killed on the spot. Another three soldiers suffered serious injury, including Joseph, whose legs were so severely damaged that the doctors had no choice but to amputate them.

Quite apart from his pain and loss, Joseph was soon confronted with society that was incapable of dealing with the disabled. He said: "My friends would come to visit, sustain fifteen minutes of artificial cheer and depart without once meeting my eye. Mother would come and cry, and it was I, who so desperately needed consolation, who had to do the consoling. Father would come and sit by my bedside in silence. I didn't know which was worse—mother's tears or father's silence. Returning to my civilian profession as a welder was, of course, impossible, and while people were quick to offer charity; no one had a job for a man without legs.

"When I ventured out in my wheelchair, people kept their distance, so that a large empty space opened around me on the busiest street corner."

Later, when Joseph met with other disabled veterans, he found that they had all had similar experiences. They had sacrificed their bodies in defense of their country, but the country, it seemed, lacked the spiritual courage to deal with the consequences of their sacrifice!

"In the summer of 1976," Joseph continued, "the Israeli Defense Force sponsored a tour of the United States for a large group of disabled veterans. While we were in New York, a member of the Chassidic Lubavitch group came to our hotel and suggested that we meet with the Lubavitcher Rebbe. Most of us did not know what to make of the invitation, but a few members of our group had heard about the Rebbe and convinced the rest of us to accept.

"As soon as they heard we were coming, the Chabadniks (as the Lubavitch members are called) sprang into action organizing the whole thing with the precision of a military campaign. Ten large commercial vans pulled up to our hotel to transport us and our wheelchairs to the Chabad headquarters in Brooklyn.

"Soon we found ourselves in the famous large synagogue in the basement of 770 Eastern Parkway. Ten minutes later, a white bearded man of about seventy entered the room, followed by two secretaries. As if by a common signal, absolute silence pervaded the room. There was no mistaking the authority he radiated. We had all stood in the presence of military commanders and prime ministers, but this was unlike anything we had ever encountered. This must have been what people felt in the presence of royalty. An identical thought passed through all our minds: Here walks a leader, a prince. He passed between us, resting his glance on each one of us and lifting his hand in greeting, and then seated himself opposite us. Again he looked at each of us in turn. Since that terrible day when

I awoke without my legs in the Rambam Hospital, I have seen all sorts of things in the eyes of those who looked at me: pain, pity, revulsion and anger. But, this was the first time in all those years that I encountered true empathy. With that glance that lasted barely a second, and with that faint smile on his lips, the Rebbe conveyed to me that he is with me utterly and exclusively.

"The Rebbe began to speak, first apologizing for his Ashkenazic accented Hebrew. He spoke about our 'disability,' saying that he objected to the use of the term: 'If a person has been deprived of a limb or a faculty,' he told us, 'this itself indicates that G-d has given him special powers to overcome the limitations this entails and to surpass the achievements of ordinary people. You are not *disabled* or *handicapped,* but special and unique, as you possess potentials that the rest of us do not. I therefore suggest that you should no longer be called *N'chei Yisroel* (crippled of Israel) our designation in the IDF bureaucracy, but *Metzuyanei Yisroel* (special ones of Israel).' "

The Rebbe continued to speak for a little while longer, and every thing he said, and more importantly, the way in which he said it, seemed to address the deep pain Joseph had been experiencing.

As they parted, the Rebbe gave each veteran a dollar bill, explaining that they should give it to charity on his behalf, making them partners in the fulfillment of a *mitzvah*. He walked from wheelchair to wheelchair, shaking each of the veterans' hands, giving them each a dollar, and adding a personal word or two.

"When my turn came," Joseph recalled, "I saw his face up close and I felt like a child. He gazed deeply into my eyes took my hand between his own, pressed it firmly, and said, 'Thank you,' with a slight nod of his head.

"I later learned that he had said something different to each one of us. To me he said, 'Thank you.' Somehow, he sensed that was exactly what I needed to hear. With those two words, the Rebbe erased all the bitterness and despair that had accumulated in my heart.

"I carried the Rebbe's 'Thank you' back to Israel, and I carry it with me to this very day."[30]

Undaunted

The poet John Milton was totally blind, but refused to be 'handicapped' by his blindness, writing the masterpieces *Paradise Lost* and

---

[30] Retold from Yosef Jacobson, "The Rebbe and the Israeli War Veterans," *Jewish Spark Magazine*. The Rebbe is quoted verbatim.

Paradise Regained in spite of it. Beethoven was deaf when he composed some of his greatest symphonies. Franklin Delano Roosevelt rose to the office of President of the United States, one of the most difficult jobs in the world, at one of the most crucial moments in history, while almost entirely paralyzed in his legs.

Sparks of Wisdom

If you have ever used a GPS System, then you are familiar with the phenomenon of making a wrong turn and having the GPS call out, "Recalculating . . . recalculating." It then provides you with a new set of directions to fix the mistake that you made. This same idea can be applied to our lives; for there are times when we feel we have made a 'wrong turn' and are now faced with difficult situations that have changed the circumstances of our lives. At such times, instead of falling into despair, we must 'recalculate' the way we are living our lives and come up with a new set of 'directions' for our new life.

Don't hold onto the pain of difficult experiences.
Let them go and figure out how to live your life
Beautifully under your new circumstances.

IV

*"When you judge a person,
give them the benefit of the doubt."*
— Rabbi Yehoshua ben Perahiah[31]

Point-of-View

> A woman was telling her friend about her children's marriages, saying: "My son has the worst marriage. Can you believe it—every morning before work he has to cook breakfast for his wife and serve it to her in bed."
>
> "But," she continued, "my daughter was more fortunate—she has a wonderful marriage. Every morning before her husband goes to work, he cooks her breakfast and serves it to her in bed."[32]

Sparks of Wisdom

The most common causes for arguments are different points-of-view, and the failure to consider other perspectives.

---

[31] Mishnah, Avot 1:6.

[32] A well-known joke.

Whenever you feel you have been mistreated, make certain you have carefully analyzed the situation before you make a final judgment. Take a moment to ask yourself a few of the following questions:

Are there perhaps other ways of looking at the situation besides my own?

Is it possible that the people who caused me pain did not know the extent of the hurt they were causing?

Were they under stress or feeling pressure to act in the way that they did?

Do they have any personal issues which make it difficult for them to do better?

Just to be clear, everyone is responsible for their own actions, even if they are under pressure, etc. However, it is easier to forgive them if we understand all the factors of the situation.

Be careful of hasty judgments.

The Art of Giving

I

The word philanthropy is derived from the Greek, philein, *meaning, 'to love,' and* athropos, *which means, 'man.' It is 'love of man.' But the Hebrew word* tzedokah *means, 'justice,' the obligation to do the right thing.*

Road Work

Chessed Halberstam worked in the employ of Rebbetzin Chaya Mushka Schneersohn, wife of the Lubavitcher Rebbe, for eighteen years—from 1970 until the Rebbetzin's passing in 1988—performing household chores and serving as the Rebbetzin's driver. Later on, he told this story of her:

I used to take the Rebbetzin out each day for fresh air. We would drive out to a park in Long Island. When my son, Ari (may G-d avenge his blood!) was a child, we would often drive by his school on Ocean Parkway and take him along; the Rebbetzin enjoyed playing with him and pushing him on the swing in the park.

One day, as we neared the park, we found our regular route closed due to road work and were forced to proceed on a parallel street. As we drove along that street, we heard the sound of a woman screaming in Russian. When I stopped at the next traffic light, the Rebbetzin turned to me and said: "My father taught me that everything a person sees is purposely orchestrated by G-d. I heard a woman screaming; can you go back and see what that was about?"

So we drove back, and there we found a woman standing on the curb and weeping while men carried furniture and other items from a house and loaded them on to a truck belonging to the county marshal. At the Rebbetzin's request, I parked behind the marshal's truck and went to learn the details of what was going on. The marshal explained that the woman had not paid her rent for many months and was now being evicted from her home.

When I told the Rebbetzin what I had heard, she asked me to go back and inquire how much the woman owed, and if he would accept a personal check; she also told me that I should not say anything to the family being evicted. At this point, I did not realize where all this was leading, but I fulfilled the Rebbetzin's request. The sum that the family owed was approximately $8,000. The marshal said that he had no problem accepting a personal check as long as he could confirm the availability of funds with the bank; he also said that if all was well with the check, his men would carry everything back into the house. When I told this to the Rebbetzin, she took out her checkbook and, to my amazement, wrote out a check for the full amount and asked me to give it to the marshal.

The marshal made a phone call to the bank and soon after instructed his workers to take everything back into the house. The Rebbetzin immediately urged me to drive away quickly before the woman realized what had transpired.[33]

Sparks of Wisdom

In the world in which we live, there are many people who have different types of difficulties. Often, we don't take the time to consider the difference we might make in someone else's life. It is a privilege to do so, and a responsibility. If G-d put us in the position to help, then we are surely expected to do so.

Kindness is both a privilege and a responsibility.

---

[33] This story is well-known in Chabad circles. A version of it exists on Chabad.org and another version may have been published before in *Kfar Chabad Magazine*.

II

*"When you are good to others,
you are best to yourself."*
— Benjamin Franklin

The Mountain Climber

A story is told of a traveler crossing the mountains in the dead of winter. He was freezing as the fierce winds blew against his face and could no longer feel his fingers or toes. When night came, he struggled against the urge to sleep, knowing that if he did, he would surely freeze to death. But he was losing hope. Finally, unable to feel his limbs, he lay down in the snow to die. But suddenly, he was seized by ay an urge to fight for his life. He stood up and decided to move on.

In pain, he started to walk against the wind when his foot immediately struck against a heap lying under the snow in his path. He bent down and pushed the snow aside and found a man there. The man had given up and lay half buried and frozen. He picked him up and started to rub the man's limbs fiercely. Soon, he saw it was working! The man opened his eyes. Together, they kept each other moving and warm until dawn. When the sun rose, the two friends were both alive.[34]

The effort to restore another to life brought warmth and energy back to the man. And this energy saved two lives.

Doing Good vs. Feeling Good

Rabbi Dr. Abraham Twerski, founder of the Gateway Rehabilitation Center in Pittsburgh, told the following story:

Once he was privileged to participate in a tribute dinner honoring a group of volunteers. They were people of all ages who had formed a group to provide companionship to 'shut-ins,' people who are essentially confined to their homes or apartments. Often, these are elderly people whose families do not live nearby, and because of poor health, poor vision, arthritis, or some such condition, are confined to their homes. Thus, these volunteers commit a few hours each week to spending time with them, taking them to the

---

[34] Retold from Jack Duweck, *The Hesed Boomerang*, Deal, New Jersey: Yagdil Torah Publications, 1998.

supermarket or the doctor's office, or for a get-together with friends.

On the tables at the tribute dinner were brochures which announced the topic of the evening, "Doing Good vs. Feeling Good." This hit home for Rabbi Twerski. After all, he was also a doctor who spent all day with people addicted to drugs and alcohol primarily because they wanted to 'feel good.' What if they could be motivated to 'do good' and allowed 'feeling good' to become of secondary importance? Could this become a treatment for chemical dependency?

The more he thought about it, the more he was convinced that he was on the right track. One may not get a 'rush' or a sudden 'high' from doing good the way one does with drugs, but the good feeling lasts longer and is more satisfying.[35]

Sparks of Wisdom

Helping people is a powerful experience, and for those who do so, it often turns into a passion. When you help someone else, besides becoming a better person, you also share in the joy you have brought to them.

---

[35] Retold from Abraham J. Twerski, *It's Not As Tough At Home as You Think*, Brooklyn, New York: Shaar Press, 1999.

The story above about the mountain climber is a metaphor for life. Sometimes people experience a harsh reality which causes them to feel that they cannot go on. But if at these difficult times, they can get involved in helping others, they might find that they have helped two people instead of just one.

If you make acts of kindness a deliberate part of your life, it can change your life. One way to do this is by keeping a 'kindness notebook,' challenging yourself to make an entry once a day. This will help you stay focused on what is really important.

Make the experience of helping people
A major part of your life.

III

*"What I gave, I have;
what I spent, I had;
what I kept, I lost."*

The Turning Point

Mr. Hershey Friedman is a successful businessman, well known for his many philanthropic endeavors. He tells the following story:

When I finished school, I entered my parent's textile business and was quite successful. Then, in the beginning of the 1980s, there was a terrible recession and interest rates rose to 22%. It became impossible to turn a profit, and it looked like I would have to close.

It was during this period that an acquaintance approached me and told me that his business would fail if I couldn't give him a loan. I had only five thousand dollars left in savings, and I didn't want to part with it . . . *but I did*. That was a turning point in my life.

Soon, a major textile company—much larger than my own—came along and essentially told me that they were buying me out and named a ridiculously low price. I refused, and they said, "We have no other choice then but to force you out of business."

Well that did it; I love a challenge. They were maybe ten times bigger than I was, but I decided to take them on. I immediately lowered my prices by 10%, undercutting them significantly and making it difficult for them to do business. My prices were simply too low.

They came back, somewhat humbled, and asked me to name my price. I did and they agreed to it. I was too young to retire, so I used the money to purchase a plastic plant.[36]

That business spawned many others and today, there are few industries in which Mr. Hershey has not been involved.

The 'Help' Returned

In Brooklyn, there is an organization called Hilf. *Hilf* is Yiddish for 'help,' and this

---

[36] Retold from *Mishpacha Magazine,* Brooklyn, New York Edition: July 1st, 2009.

organization does great work in Brooklyn; they find sick or elderly people who are unable to cook for themselves and arrange for volunteers to cook the meals and deliver them.

One of the Hilf volunteers is Leah Freund, who cooks a meal every Tuesday night. One Monday, Leah received a call from Hilf saying that the driver who usually picks up her meal cannot make it . . . Would she be able to deliver the meal herself? Leah answered, "Of course," and took down the home address of the woman.

On Tuesday, Leah cooked the meal and delivered it. As she was about to, leave the woman said to her, "You look familiar, please stay and talk a few minutes; perhaps it will come to me why you seem so familiar." So Leah stayed to talk.

After a few minutes, the elderly woman asked her, "Are you by any chance Tzila's daughter.

Leah was surprised and said, "Yes."

"I knew you looked familiar," the elderly woman said, "you look just as your mother did when she was younger. Sit down and I will tell you something interesting."

Then the old woman related the following story:

"During the War, your mother and I were both inmates in the Bergen-Belsen concentration camp, and we were slowly starving to death. One day, your mother was not doing well—her face was white, she couldn't take the hunger—and she asked me for some of my rations. I broke off a small piece of bread from my small piece and gave it to her, and immediately she felt better. She could not stop thanking me, and said over and over again, 'If I survive the War, I will never forget what you did for me, and I will repay you for the kindness you have shown me.'

After the War—which we both, thank G-d, survived—your mother never forgot the kindness I showed her and sometimes reminds me how indebted she feels to me."

The woman then turned to Leah and asked, "Don't you think its amazing that now, when I have reached a age when I need help with food, it is Tzila's daughter who is providing it for me?"[37]

Sparks of Wisdom

Sometimes we find it difficult to help someone because, to do so, would require a large commitment, either financially or emotionally. At

---
[37] I heard the story from my father who heard it from Leah Freund.

such times, we should consider how G-d might be using us for His ends, and how the blessing of the act will more than compensate for the obstacles we must overcome.

When you give,
You get back more.

The Art of Faith

I

"Happiness is attained through the three F's—Friends, Family, and Faith."
— David Pelcovitz

Afraid of Faith

Once, a writer who came to see the Rebbe pointed out how many non-believers there were in the world. The Rebbe disagreed with him, saying: "People are natural believers. There may be doubts; to question G-d, however, is the first indication that one believes in something. You must have some acceptance of G-d even to question Him."

"But if they believe, why don't they act on it?" the writer asked.

The Rebbe replied: "They are afraid of their faith. They fear the demands their faith might put upon them, that they might have to forgo some of their comfort, or compromise some of their ideas. They fear changing their lives."[38]

Belief in G-d

---

[38] Retold from Jacobson, *Towards a Meaningful Life,* 224-225. The Rebbe is quoted verbatim.

After losing a child in a tragic car accident, a father reflects on his faith:

Oh my G-d, it hurts so much. Boruch, Boruch—why did you go away? . . . We miss you so . . . Let it all be a dream from which I'll wake up soon . . . It cannot be true . . . Things like that should not happen . . . How can a *loving* G-d allow this?

I believe in G-d. It is not what people call blind faith. I believe in the Creator in various ways. I *feel* that He exists. And I *understand* that He exists. It is good—and sometimes necessary—to support our faith with rational arguments, especially at a time like this. For I know that parents in similar circumstances have lost their faith. So I find it good to consider again, one by one, the reasons for my belief in G-d.

I have often dealt with this subject, when talking to others. I have explained that we believe in a Higher Being based on various logical reasoning.

For example, nothing in the world comes into being by itself. That means, as well, that the world in its totality has not come into being by itself. There is a *Generator*.

The more the scientists—biologists, biochemists, ecologists, nuclear physicists, mathematicians—penetrate into the mysteries of the micro- and macro-cosmos, the more they become convinced that this incredibly ingenious system is the work of a *Super-Organizer/Designer*.

"Man and matter are not composed of tangible substance, but of entirely elusive processes without a clear boundary between spirit and matter. Scientifically, it appears that spirit and body, time and space, universe and atom are all aspects of one Reality which to an ever increasing degree appear to be one great Thought."

Actually, everybody is a believer. Even those who claim to have no faith are believers. For "to believe" means to accept and acknowledge something that cannot be known. There are things in the world which cannot be known, or can be known only partially. Yet we do accept their existence. For we understand that human reason is not the only criterion for deciding whether something exists or not. And we accept its existence, not because we can prove it absolutely, but because it is very plausible, and indeed evident, beyond denial. In this manner, reason may go far to make the existence of G-d plausible and highly probable. It is extremely improbable that G-d does *not* exist.

People who deny His existence say that they do not believe. But this formula is simply wrong. They do believe: they believe in the

> non-existence of G-d. And just as I believe in His existence and try to make this plausible and highly probable—virtually evident—so too a person who believes in the Creator's non-existence must equally find ways to support his view with ironclad arguments. He too must explain the origin and organization of the world. He cannot evade this task.
>
> It is not enough for him to declare that science will eventually explain all this. And if he does declare this, he merely shows that, in this way, he too, is a believer.[39]

Sparks of Wisdom

The subject of faith is truly vast, and thus it is not possible to treat it in any complete way in this small chapter. However, as the focus of this book is on how to live well and create the foundations for a happy life, I will venture to say that faith is the foundation for living well.

We live in a world where we are constantly challenged by obstacles and opportunities that clash with healthy spiritual and holistic human values. Often, the opportunities are truly enticing. This is where faith comes in; for it serves as an inspiration and provides us with the tools to make the right decisions and to carry them through in a most successful manner. When

---

[39] Reprinted with permission from Yitzchok Vorst, *Why, Reflections on the Loss of a Loved One*, 47-49.

we have G-d in our lives, we are connected to a reality that is infinitely greater than our own isolated perception of things. This affects us in a strong way; it warms our hearts, brings us meaning, and elevates all of our life experiences. As a result, we are better equipped to make proper choices in life, and to carry them through successfully.

Apart from *being* an inspiration for good living, faith also *pushes* us into good living. As human beings with weaknesses, we are often vulnerable to making the wrong decision. One of the things that keeps people on the right track is the knowledge that they will be held responsible for their actions. However, many times people bypass their fear of being held responsible by telling themselves that no one will find out what they are doing. However, when one has faith in a Creator who knows all, then the knowledge that we will ultimately be held responsible for our actions will often steer us away from the wrong decision.[40]

A relationship with G-d
Is the best foundation for a successful life.

---

[40] Judaism teaches that in the Torah, which is the body of Law for the Jewish people, there is also a set of laws for the nations of the world. These are called the Seven Noachide laws, and they include: 1. Do not worship idols, believe in G-d; 2. Do not blaspheme His Name, respect G-d and Praise Him; 3. Do not murder, respect human life; 4. Do not commit immoral sexual acts, respect the family; 5. Do not steal, respect the rights and property of others; 6. Pursue justice, create a judicial system; and 7. Do not eat the flesh of an animal while it is still alive, respect all creatures.

Bibliography

Abramov, Yirmiyohu, and Tehilla Abramov. *Two Halves of a Whole*. Southfield, Michigan: Targum Press, 1994.

Country Yossi Family Magazine. Brooklyn, New York: December, 2009.

Duweck, Jack. *The Hesed Boomerang*. Deal, New Jersey: Yagdil Torah Publications, 1998.

Goldwasser, Dovid. *It Happened in Heaven*. Nanuet, New York: Feldheim Publishers, 1995.

Jacobson, Simon, ed.. *Towards a Meaningful Life*. Brooklyn, New York: William Morrow and Co., 1995.

Jacobson, Yosef. "The Rebbe and the Israeli War Veterans." *Jewish Spark Magazine,* Vol. 5, Issue 3, September 1999.

Jungreis, Esther. *The Committed Marriage*. New York: Harper Collins Publishers, 2002.

———. "Rebbetzin's Viewpoint." *The Jewish Press,* Brooklyn, New York.

Mandel, Morris. *Stories to Live By*. Jerusalem: [no publisher], 2004.

———. "Youth Speaks Up." *The Jewish Press*. Brooklyn, New York: [no date].

Mandel, Morris, and Aaron J. Novick. *Walk With Me to Happiness*. Jerusalem: [no publisher], 2001.

Majeski, Shloma. *The Chassidic Approach to Joy*. Brooklyn, New York: Sichos in English, 1995.

Nshei Chabad Newsletter. [no city]: [no publisher], [no date].

Paley, Eliyahu, Ed.. *Mishpacha Magazine,* Brooklyn, New York: July 1,

2009.

———. *Mishpacha Magazine*. Brooklyn, New York: April 28, 2010.

Patterson, Kerry, Joseph Grenny, Al Switzler, and Ron Macmillan. *The Balancing Act: Mastering the Competing Demands of Leadership*. Cincinnati, Ohio: Thompson Executive Press Division of Southwestern College Publishing, 1996.

Twerski, Abraham J.. *Forgiveness: Don't Let Resentment Keep You Captive*. Brooklyn, New York: Shaar Press, 2012.

———. *Happiness and the Human Spirit: The Spirituality of Becoming the Best You Can Be*. Woodstock, Vermont: Jewish Lights Publishing, 2007.

———. *It's Not As Tough At Home as You Think*. Brooklyn, New York: Shaar Press, 1999.

———. *Visions of the Fathers*. Brooklyn, New York: Shaar Press, 1999.

Vorst, Yitzchok. *Why, Reflections on the Loss of a Loved One*. Holland: Merkos Publications, 2007.

About the Author

Rabbi Pesach Scheiner was born in Brooklyn, New York, and received his rabbinical ordination from the Chabad-Lubavitch Yeshiva in Brooklyn. He is currently the rabbi of the Chabad Center in Boulder, Colorado. Chabad is an international organization which reaches out to Jews of all backgrounds, endeavoring to teach them about their Jewish heritage and to support them in Jewish practice. In his rabbinic capacity, Rabbi Scheiner teaches classes on Jewish practice, including the Jewish view on living successfully from which this book was born. He lives with his wife and children in Boulder, Colorado.

Made in the USA
Charleston, SC
15 May 2014